curious about

THE BERMUDA TRIANGLE

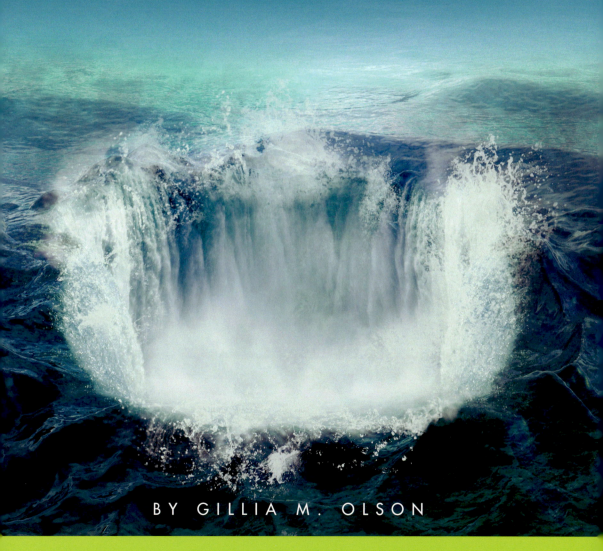

BY GILLIA M. OLSON

AMICUS LEARNING

What are you

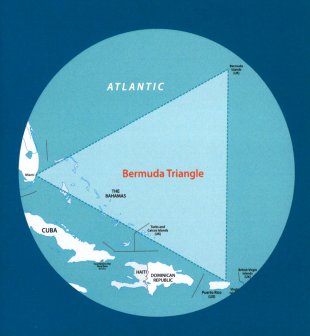

CHAPTER ONE

1

What the Bermuda Triangle Is
PAGE
4

CHAPTER TWO

2

Bermuda Triangle Stories
PAGE
10

curious about?

CHAPTER **3**

Looking for Answers
PAGE **16**

Stay Curious! Learn More . . . 22
Glossary 24
Index 24

Curious About is published by
Amicus Learning, an imprint of Amicus
P.O. Box 227
Mankato, MN 56002
www.amicuspublishing.us

Copyright © 2025 Amicus.
International copyright reserved in all countries.
No part of this book may be reproduced in any
form without written permission from the publisher.

Editor: Ana Brauer
Series Designer: Kathleen Petelinsek
Book Designer and Photo Researcher: Emily Dietz

Library of Congress Cataloging-in-Publication Data
Names: Olson, Gillia M., author.
Title: Curious about the Bermuda Triangle / by Gillia
M. Olson. Other titles: Bermuda Triangle
Description: Mankato, MN : Amicus Learning, [2025] |
Series: Curious about unexplained mysteries | Includes
bibliographical references and index. | Audience: Ages
6–9 years | Audience: Grades 2–3 | Summary: "Why
do planes and ships disappear at the Bermuda Triangle?
Learn about this unexplained mystery in this question-
and-answer book for elementary-aged readers. Includes
infographics, table of contents, glossary, books and websites
for further research, and index"— Provided by publisher.
Identifiers: LCCN 2024014745 (print) | LCCN
2024014746 (ebook) | ISBN 9798892000932
(lib bdg) | ISBN 9798892001519 (paperback)
| ISBN 9798892002097 (ebook)
Subjects: LCSH: Bermuda Triangle—Juvenile literature.
Classification: LCC G558 .O47 2025 (print) | LCC
G558 (ebook) | DDC 001.94—dc23/eng/20240508
LC record available at https://lccn.loc.gov/2024014745
LC ebook record available at https://lccn.loc.gov/2024014746

Photos Credits: Alamy Stock Photo/CBW, 8, john standing,
14–15, VICTOR HABBICK VISIONS, cover; Getty Images/
Bettmann / Contributor, 10–11, Keystone / Stringer, 2,
13, VICTOR HABBICK VISIONS, 16–17; Noun Project/
kenzi mebius, 17, MihiMihi, 22, 23, Sunisih, 22, 23,
zaenul yahya, 17; Shutterstock/littlesam, 19, Paopano,
20, Rainer Lesniewski, 2, 6–7, Viktor Hladchenko, 3,
21, Wonderful Nature, 4–5; Vecteezy/artefacti, 9

Printed in China

CHAPTER ONE

What is the Bermuda Triangle?

DID YOU KNOW?
The Bermuda Triangle is also called the Devil's Triangle.

Many people believe that the Bermuda Triangle causes ships to disappear.

The Bermuda Triangle is in the Atlantic Ocean. Boats, planes, and even people have **disappeared** there. Some people think mysterious forces make them disappear. Others say the reasons are not a mystery at all.

WHAT THE BERMUDA TRIANGLE IS

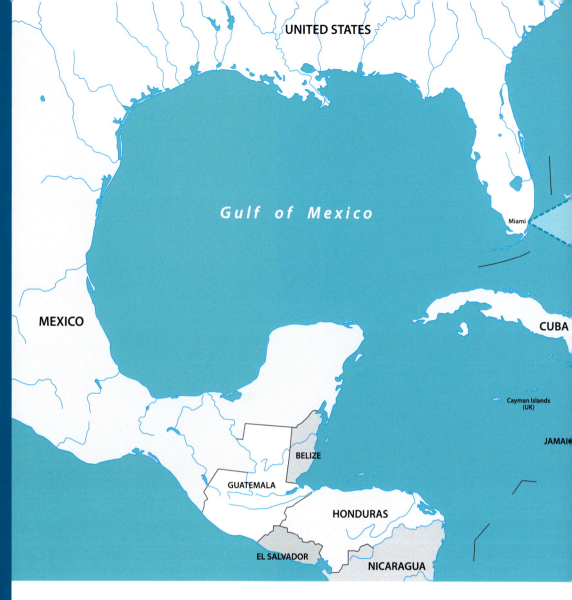

Where is it?

6

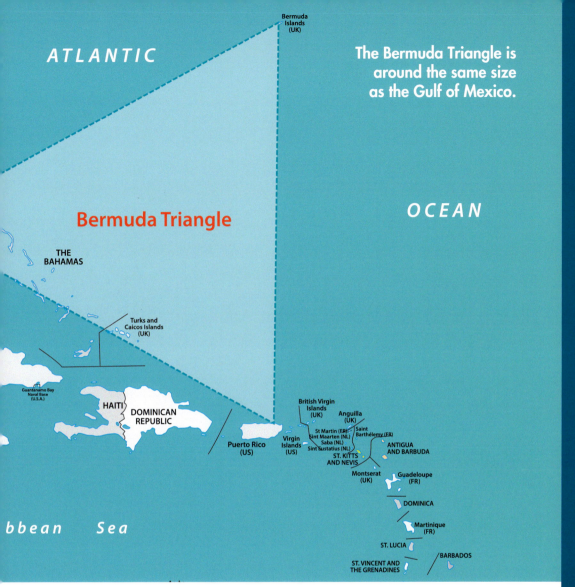

The Bermuda Triangle is shaped like a triangle. One corner is Miami, Florida. The other points are Bermuda and Puerto Rico. The deepest point of the Atlantic Ocean is there. It is 5.2 miles (8.4 kilometers) deep.

How did it get its name?

Vincent Gaddis called it the Bermuda Triangle in 1964. He wrote about planes and ships disappearing. Charles Berlitz wrote a book, *The Bermuda Triangle*, in 1974. Berlitz thought the lost city of **Atlantis** was in the Triangle. He had no **proof**. But the book was a best-seller.

DID YOU KNOW?
The Bermuda Triangle sold 14 million copies.

Could the lost city of Atlantis be in the Bermuda Triangle? Author Charles Berlitz thought it was.

WHAT THE BERMUDA TRIANGLE IS

CHAPTER TWO
2

What was the first ship to disappear?

In 1918, the U.S.S. *Cyclops* disappeared. It was a U.S. Navy cargo ship. It was going from Barbados to Baltimore, Maryland. There were 306 crew members. Its last message said the weather was good. It was never heard from again. It sent no **distress** call.

No one knows what happened to the U.S.S. *Cyclops.* It is still a mystery.

What planes have disappeared?

In 1945, Flight 19 disappeared. This training flight had five Navy bomber planes. The lead pilot said his compasses were not working. He was lost. All five planes disappeared. Rescue planes were sent out. One of them also disappeared. None of the planes have been found.

DID YOU KNOW?
The flight leader had been lost while flying before. He had to be rescued two other times.

No one knows what happened to Flight 19. Some people think they ran out of gas.

BERMUDA TRIANGLE STORIES

13

The SS *Cotopaxi* was a cargo ship that disappeared. The wreck was found 95 years later.

In 1925, the SS *Cotopaxi* was going from Charleston, South Carolina, to Havana, Cuba. Its path was through the Triangle. It disappeared on the way. In 2020, a shipwreck near Florida was later found to be the *Cotopaxi*. Experts think a sudden storm sank the ship.

LOOKING FOR ANSWERS

CHAPTER THREE

Why do things disappear there?

Some stories about the Triangle say the ocean opens and pulls ships and planes under the water.

Many things cause sinking or crashing. Most likely, bad weather or people's mistakes are the causes. Before modern weather **forecasting**, sailors often had no warning of bad weather. Storms often meet in the Triangle. Big waves, lightning, and heavy rain could cause crashes.

More than 50 ships and 20 airplanes have disappeared in the Bermuda Triangle.

LOOKING FOR ANSWERS

Why haven't people found plane wrecks?

Crashed planes can break into small pieces. These pieces will quickly sink or drift away. Even today, it's hard to find pieces from plane crashes. The ocean is very deep in the Triangle. It is hard to search.

Divers often search for proof of wrecks in the Triangle.

LOOKING FOR ANSWERS

LOOKING FOR ANSWERS

Hundreds of planes safely fly over the Triangle every year.

Is it safe to go there?

Ships and planes go through the Triangle every day. The area is a busy place. Other busy waterways have the same number of ship or plane incidents. Ships and planes do not disappear more often in the Bermuda Triangle.

The Bermuda Triangle is not any more dangerous than any other stretch of water.

LOOKING FOR ANSWERS

21

STAY CURIOUS!

ASK MORE QUESTIONS

How do people search for plane crashes?

What other places have ships disappeared?

Try a BIG QUESTION: If people found wreckage of Flight 19, what might that mean for the legend of the Bermuda Triangle?

SEARCH FOR ANSWERS

Search the library catalog or the Internet.
A librarian, teacher, or parent can help you.

Using Keywords
Find the looking glass.

Keywords are the most important words in your question.

?

If you want to know about:
- how people search for plane crashes, type: SEARCHING FOR PLANE CRASHES
- ship disappearances, type: UNEXPLAINED SHIP DISAPPEARANCES

LEARN MORE

FIND GOOD SOURCES

Here are some good, safe sources you can use in your research.
Your librarian can help you find more.

Books

Searching for Bermuda Triangle Answers
by Thomas Kingsley Troupe, 2020.

The Bermuda Triangle
by Marysa Storm, 2020.

Internet Sites

Kiddle: Bermuda Triangle Facts For Kids
https://kids.kiddle.co/Bermuda_Triangle
Kiddle is an encyclopedia for kids with facts on many topics.

Wonderopolis: Can You Survive the Bermuda Triangle?
https://wonderopolis.org/wonder/can-you-survive-the-bermuda-triangle
Wonderopolis is a non-profit site for students and their families.

Every effort has been made to ensure that these websites are appropriate for children. However, because of the nature of the Internet, it is impossible to guarantee that these sites will remain active indefinitely or that their contents will not be altered.

SHARE AND TAKE ACTION

Visit your local historical society.
Learn about the history of your town. Have any planes or boats gone missing in the area?

Learn about using directions the way sailors or pilots might do by geocaching.
This activity involves figuring out where "treasure" is using smartphone apps.

Go on a field trip to a local meteorology center, or try a virtual field trip.
Learn how weather forecasts help pilots and captains.

23

GLOSSARY

Atlantis A legendary city said to have sunk into the sea.

disappear To stop being visible; to pass out of sight.

distress In danger or in great need of help.

forecast To predict weather based on data.

proof Facts or evidence that show something is true.

INDEX

Atlantic Ocean, 5, 7
Berlitz, Charles, 8–9
Flight 19, 12–13
Florida, 7, 15
Gaddis, Vincent, 8
plane crashes, 18
safety, 20–21
shipwrecks, 15
SS *Cotopaxi*, 14–15
U.S.S. *Cyclops*, 10–11
weather, 11, 15, 17

About the Author

Gillia Olson is a skeptic by nature but loves all things paranormal. She stays curious and open-minded and hopes you will, too. She lives in southern Minnesota.